M551 Sheridan

In Action No. 2041

by David Doyle

Cover Art by Don Greer

Line Illustrations by Matheu Spraggins

Introduction

Through the years, two widely divergent schools of thought have formed on the M551 Sheridan. One camp sees the vehicle as an enormously expensive, complicated weapons system that was largely a failure. The other camp sees the Sheridan as a wholly successful system, that despite its teething problems, provided U.S. troops with an armored asset with capabilities that remain unequalled. Regardless of one's viewpoint, the fact that the Sheridan remained in front-line service with the Army for three decades makes it unique among tank designs. The forces that came together to create this design were as unique as the vehicle iteslf.

In November 1945, the War Department Equipment Board (popularly known as the Stilwell Board) set out criteria for the postwar development of army material of all types, including tanks. Against a baseline of the then current U.S. light tank, the M24 Chaffee, this report set out the design parameters of light tanks by saying: "The light tank is for reconnaissance and security. . . . The present light tank should be further developed to obtain the maximum cross-country mobility and maneuverability and all around armor protection against small arms and shell fragments, with frontal armor protection against light antitank guns. It should not exceed 25 tons in weight. The tank gun should be of approximately 3-inch caliber, capable of penetrating 5 inches of homogenous armor at 30-degree obliquity at 1,000 yards using special ammunition."

Most of these criteria echoed those of the Report of the Armored Equipment Board (Robinett Board), which generated a voluminous report at the Armor Center at Fort Knox in 1945. The Army Ground Forces Equipment Review Board (Cook Board) had come to the same conclusion in June of 1945.

Accordingly, in July of 1946 designers sat out to achieve the prescribed goals, generating a series of designs that would eventually evolve into the M41 Walker Bulldog. Although the M41 was well-liked by the crews, and was a marked improvement over the M24 Chaffee, it fell short of the lofty goals set by the Stilwell board – notably in weight and range – and thus was considered only an interim vehicle. Work continued toward meeting Stilwell Board standards, and in May 1952 the characteristics of a successor to the M41 were outlined. Although an upper weight limit of 20 tons was initially imposed, this was soon revised downward to 18 tons. By July of 1953 proposals had been received from Detroit Arsenal, the Cadillac Motor Car Division of General Motors, and Aircraft Armaments, Incorporated (AAI).

The AAI design, the T92 76mm gun tank, was selected for further development, with the first pilot model arriving at Aberdeen Proving Ground for testing in November 1956. In order to reach the design criteria, the AAI engineers had created a very compact vehicle – with less volume to protect, the shear weight of armor could be held down, with the further benefit of presenting a small target. Though not without a few bugs, testing went well and it

Acknowledgments

All photos, unless otherwise noted, are from the National Archives and Records Administration collection. The Patton Museum, the Ordnance Museum, and the Rock Island Arsenal Museum provided additional photos.

This book would not have been possible without the generous assistance of Doug Kibbey, Chris Harlow, Dave Orth, William Powis, Jim Mesko, Michael Green, and especially Denise Moss, who patiently traveled with me and copied countless photos and documents as we researched this volume.

Copyright 2008 Squadron/Signal Publications
1115 Crowley Drive, Carrollton, TX 75006-1312 U.S.A.
Printed in the U.S.A.

All rights reserved. No part of this publication may be reproduced, stored in a retrieval system, or transmitted in any form by means electrical, mechanical, or otherwise, without written permission of the publisher.

ISBN 978-0-89747-582-2

Military/Combat Photographs and Snapshots

If you have any photos of aircraft, armor, soldiers, or ships of any nation, particularly wartime snapshots, why not share them with us and help make Squadron/Signal's books all the more interesting and complete in the future? Any photograph sent to us will be copied and returned. Electronic images are preferred. The donor will be fully credited for any photos used. Please send them to:

Squadron/Signal Publications
1115 Crowley Drive
Carrollton, TX 75006-1312 U.S.A.
www.SquadronSignalPublications.com

About the In Action® Series

In Action® books, despite the title of the genre, are books that trace the development of a single type of aircraft, armored vehicle, or ship from prototype to the final production variant. Experimental or "one-off" variants can also be included. Our first *In Action®* book was printed in 1971.

(Title Page) The M551 Sheridan Armored Reconnaissance/Airborne Assault Vehicle was conceived in 1959, produced in the 1960s, and saw combat into the 1990s. Although the M551 had its shortcomings, a suitable replacement has yet to be found. (Patton Museum)

(Front Cover) The M551 first served in Vietnam and into the 1990s. Intended as a fast reconnaissance vehicle with potent tank-killing abilities, the Sheridan's 152mm round proved effective against infantry and fortifications.

(Back Cover) The 82nd Airborne Division operated the M551A1 Sheridan in the Mid-East during Operation Desert Storm, which was the Sheridan's last combat deployment, bringing down the curtain on three decades of service.

This 3rd Squadron, 4th Cavalry, 25th Infantry Division vehicle in Vietnam has had its turret ventilator relocated to the top left of its turret. Located on the left rear side of the turret on early vehicles, the ventilator was moved to the turret's top left on later production vehicles. Barely visible is a second M2 machine gun, which the 65th Engineers added to this unit's vehicles. The 65th Engineers also fabricated the bustle stowage racks. In smooth conditions the Sheridan had an approximate cruising range of 350 miles.

was anticipated that the T92 would enter production in 1962. In 1957, however, all of these well-laid plans would change.

A Congressional committee looking at military matters noted that the Soviet Union was also outfitting its force with a new light tank – but theirs was amphibious. The obvious question was, why was America's new light tank not also amphibious? In order for an object to float, it must weigh less than an equal volume of water (displacement). Here the compact design of the T92 became its undoing – with its small volume and relatively high mass, not only would it not float, it could not reasonably be made to float. In June 1958 further development of the T92 was cancelled, and the engineers returned to their drawing boards seeking to create a vehicle that not only met the Stilwell requirements, but was also amphibious.

Coincidentally, along the way the method used by the U.S. Army to classify tanks was changed. First, on 9 November 1950, tanks were no longer to be classified by weight, but rather by main gun caliber. Thus, the T41E1 Light Tank became the 76mm gun tank T41E1, which then became the M41. Then, in August 1957 an even more wide sweeping approach was taken. For future tank developments, it was mandated that the U.S. would have one type of tank – classified as the Main Battle Tank. Gone were light, medium, heavy, 76mm, 90mm, 120mm etc., tank designations. To augment the Main Battle Tank there would also be the Armored Reconnaissance/Airborne Assault Vehicle. Because of this, the vehicle that was to replace the aborted T92 project was an Armored Reconnaissance/Airborne Assault Vehicle (AR/AAV).

Specifications for the new vehicle were presented to industry in July 1959, and in October of the same year two of the twelve responses were selected for further study. One design came from AAI, and the other from Cadillac, which in 1948 had been selected as the primary producer of light tanks in the event of a future national emergency. In 1960 a contract was awarded to Cadillac for further development of its design, which was designated the XM551. The name General Sheridan was approved by the Secretary of the Army in August of 1961.

The Cadillac Armored Reconnaissance/Airborne Assault Vehicle met the army requirements of being both amphibious and air droppable. Despite its lengthy official nomenclature, to the casual observer, and most in the military – it was a tank. The Allison Division of General Motors built 1,562 of these tanks beginning in 1966, with the last Sheridan rolling off the Cleveland assembly line in 1970.

The primary armament – and coincidentally the primary source of trouble for the vehicle – was the 152mm gun/launcher that could fire either conventional ammunition or the Ford-built Shillelagh anti-tank missile. The problem with the "conventional" ammunition was that it was not conventional at all. Rather than a metal cartridge case, the Sheridan's ammunition (which it also shared with the M60A2 "Starship") had combustible cartridge cases. The nature of these cases was such that they had to be protected from moisture – even humidity – in order that they stay together and completely burn. A removable bag system was developed, with the loader stripping the bag off just as the round was chambered. The relatively fragile rounds also posed a distinct fire and explosion hazard for the crew.

The 152mm gun/launcher was designed primarily as a missile launcher, with the gun aspect being secondary. The Sheridan fired the Shillelagh missile in combat only in Desert Storm, and then fewer than a half-dozen missiles were fired, in contrast to the thousands of rounds of conventional munitions expended in Vietnam, Panama, and Desert Storm. With a big bore and no muzzle brake on the short barrel, when conventional rounds were fired often the first one or two road wheel positions would lift from the ground from the recoil.

In order to keep weight to a minimum, a necessity for the Sheridan's airborne and amphibious requirements, the M551 hull was made of welded 7039 aluminum alloy armor plate. The turret, however, was made from steel armor. A layer of high-density foam encased the basic hull. This was an effort to improve floatation. Around the foam thin aluminum skin clad the exterior of the hull. A 6-cylinder Detroit Diesel engine powered the vehicle.

As early as 1966 there began to be rumblings about deploying the new vehicle to Vietnam – in part as a "field trial." However, persistent problems with the combustible case ammunition and the lack of viable targets for the expensive Shillelagh missile postponed this deployment. Finally, with the bugs worked out, in 1968 the decision was made to equip the 3rd Squadron, 4th Cavalry and 1st Squadron, 11th Armored Cavalry Regiment with the Sheridan. Both units were already serving in Vietnam. For the 11th ACR, who up to this time had been using the M113 armored personnel carrier, this was a definite upgrade – however, the troopers in the 3rd Squadron, 4th Cavalry were trading in heavily armed and armored M48A3 Patton tanks for the lightweight Sheridans. Nonetheless, these two units employed the Sheridan admirably and effectively, accumulating far more combat hours in the vehicles than any other units.

The tank that wasn't - the T92 76 mm gun tank was created in the late 1950s to be America's next generation light tank. Its lack of amphibious capabilities, along with the need for a larger weapon, led to its cancellation and the subsequent development of the M551 Sheridan. (TACOM LCMC History Office)

Two proposals were given serious consideration for the Armored Reconnaissance/ Airborne Assault Vehicle (AR/AAV) contract. One was a joint effort by Aircraft Armaments Incorporated and Allis Chalmers, while the other was submitted by the Cadillac Motor Car Division of General Motors. The Cadillac proposal was accepted, with this being one of the early concept drawings. (TACOM LCMC History Office)

Designated the XM551, the first pilot model of the AR/AAV was delivered in June 1962. While the basic shape of the aluminum-hulled vehicle had been defined, the evolution of the design is far from complete. Notice the band-type track. (TACOM LCMC History Office)

The style of the fourth pilot model, now preserved at the Patton Museum, defined the shape of the Sheridan. Conventional track has replaced band track, and larger, 24 1/2-inch diameter roadwheels have been used. The surfboard, intended to prevent swamping during amphibious operations, has been deployed in this view. (David Doyle)

Pilot number five was essentially identical to pilot four, and like its predecessors, had a conventional-style driver's hatch on the centerline of the hull. The XM551 was powered by a Detroit Diesel 6V53 engine. The early pilots, including this one, had water jet propulsion for amphibious operations. A power take off (PTO) from the Allison XTG-250 transmission drove the water jet propulsion unit. (TACOM LCMC History Office)

With the seventh XM551 pilot, shown here, the front of the vehicle was heavily restyled, and a rotating driver's hatch replaced the conventional unit. This design gave the driver excellent visibility without requiring him to lift his head above the plane of the hull. The "hub caps" visible on the road wheels were an effort to improve buoyancy. A 15mm XM122 spotting rifle is mounted adjacent to the 152mm gun/launcher. (Rock Island Arsenal Museum)

XM551 pilots 9 through 11 were delivered in 1964 and utilized in the engineering/service test program, primarily at Aberdeen Proving Ground, Maryland. Below is a shot of pilot 10, shown test firing the 152mm gun/launcher. (TACOM LCMC History Office)

XM551 pilot seven was tested extensively at Aberdeen Proving Ground. With the seventh pilot, the road wheel diameter increased yet again, this time to 28 inches in diameter, the size it would remain during series production. Beginning with this pilot, the water jet propulsion system was eliminated. (TACOM LCMC History Office)

With the 12th XM551 pilot, shown here, delivered February 1965, the vehicle was fully defined. The most notable difference between this and the earlier pilots was the new two-piece folding surfboard and a folding flotation barrier, seen here stowed on the top edges of the hull. (TACOM LCMC History Office)

A Shillelagh missile leaves the muzzle of Pilot 12 during October 1967 testing. Various versions of the Shillelagh were produced, with the standard variant, the MGM51A, carrying 8 pounds of Octol explosives and having a range of about 2000 meters. It is believed that the destruction of an Iraqi anti-tank gun with a single such missile during Operation Desert Storm is the sole combat victory by the Ford-built Shillelagh. (U.S. Army Engineer School History Office)

A Shillelagh is launched from Pilot 12 at night. Night sighting of the 152mm gun/launcher remained problematic until 1990 when a handful of vehicles were fitted with the Tank Thermal Sight (TTS) from the M60A3. (Patton Museum)

The first 730 meters of missile flight were unguided, after which the missile was guided by an infrared link to the gunner's sight. The missile tracked to the point on which the gunner's crosshairs were trained until detonation. (Patton Museum)

The erected configuration of the flotation barrier is displayed on pilot 12. Obviously, the fabric barrier was easily damaged. The hull of the vehicle itself was the greatest source of buoyancy. Ahead of the gun barrel can be seen the upper of two visors provided for the driver in the screen. (Patton Museum)

Pilots and early production M551s featured an open breech scavenging system and bore evacuator. This system blew burning debris into the vehicle (possibly igniting stowed ammo), and led to a closed breech scavenging system (CBSS) that was factory installed beginning with vehicle 700 and retrofitted to earlier vehicles.

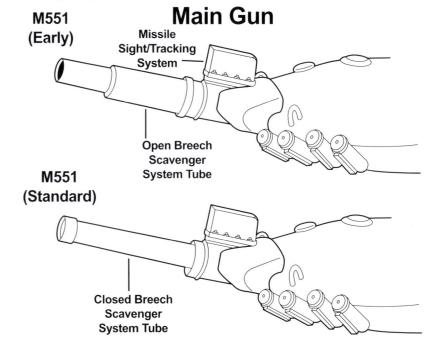

The production contract for the Sheridan was awarded to the Allison Division of General Motors on 12 April 1965. The vehicle was classified Standard A in May 1966, and the following month the first two production vehicles were delivered. This is the 24th production vehicle, and was photographed at Aberdeen Proving Ground shortly after its 1966 delivery. (Ordnance Museum)

The collapsible floatation barrier was stowed around the upper perimeter of the vehicle hull. The extensive stenciling on the turret of this example denotes where various pieces of On Vehicle Material (OVM) were to be stored. (Ordnance Museum)

Though conceived primarily as a rapidly-deployable reconnaissance vehicle/tank killer on a feared European battlefield, the Sheridan is most often remembered for its use in Vietnam. This 3rd Squadron, 4th Cavalry, 25th Infantry Division M551 was photographed on Range 3 at Cu Chi, Vietnam, on 1 February 1969 - the crew's last day of training.

Fifty-four Sheridans were shipped to Vietnam in January 1969. The missile systems were left behind because there were few or no suitable targets for the expensive missiles. Operating in concert with the M113 as here, the M551 was widely used in the reconnaissance role.

As with any AFV, stowage space on the M551 was at a premium. The large bustle basket fitted to this Troop "A," 11th Armored Cavalry Sheridan in 1969 was a typical field expedient to address this problem. This photo was snapped as A Troop patrolled the area around Long Binh.

Along with M113 Armored Personnel Carriers (APCs), M551 Airborne Armored Reconnaissance Vehicles from Troop "A," 11th Armored Cavalry, move out during a sweep of the Long Binh area.

Among the items stowed in the turret bustle rack of this 11th Armored Cavalry M551, photographed in 1969, are several cots and, worthy of note, a pair of plastic jerry cans. Additional cots are stowed on the rear of the engine deck of the vehicle as well, along with a plethora of other gear, including a number of spare track links.

Two Sheridans from 2nd Platoon, "C" Troop, 1st Squadron, 11th Armored Cavalry pause during operations in 1969. In order to protect the vehicle commanders, who often rode in open hatches, against small arms fire, troopers first adapted components from the M113 ACAV kit to the Sheridan, as is the case with these vehicles. (*Armor Magazine*)

Combat Modifications

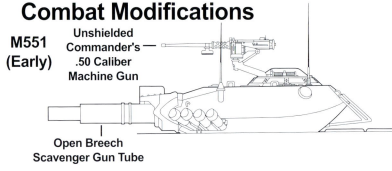

M551 (Early) — Unshielded Commander's .50 Caliber Machine Gun; Open Breech Scavenger Gun Tube

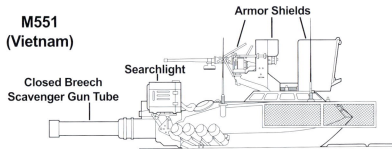

M551 (Vietnam) — Armor Shields; Searchlight; Closed Breech Scavenger Gun Tube

Frequent close-quarters encounters with enemy infantry in Vietnam led to the creation of the Commander's Ballistic Shield Kit, dubbed the "birdcage" by troops.

Soldiers of Troop "B," 3rd Squadron, 14th Cavlary, 25th Infantry Division, strap newly-issued pioneer tools on the rear deck of an M551 at Cu Chi on 27 January 1969. The extensive white stenciling noting what gear is to be stowed where is readily apparent. These were among the first 54 Sheridans to arrive in Vietnam earlier in the month.

The heavy brush encountered in Vietnam, such as this being pushed through by Troop "A," 11th Armored Cavalry, lead to overheating problems, transmission wear, and considerable maintenance effort.

This row of new M551 Air Droppable Assault Vehicles had only been in country a few days when photographed at Cu Chi on 24 January 1969. Belonging to the 3rd Squadron, 4th Cavalry, 25th Infantry Division, they are already covered in dust.

Sheridan crews of the 3rd Squadron, 4th Cavalry, 25th Infantry Division line up on the range at Cu Chi to fire their 152mm main guns on 1 February 1969. The semi-gloss nature of the FS-595A 24087 olive drab paint, standard for U.S. Army vehicles during the Vietnam era, is clear.

But for the chain-link fence anti-RPG screens, these "B" Troop, 3rd Squadron, 4th Cavalry, 25th Infantry Division Sheridans appear factory-new in this 12 February 1969 photo. Within days, however, the crews would begin adding a potpourri of gear, and operations in Vietnam would coat the vehicles in dust and scratch the paint.

Small pieces of chain-link fencing have been attached to jury-rigged supports on the front of this M551. This was an effort to protect the Sheridan from RPGs. RPGs and mines proved the greatest threat to U.S. armored vehicles in Vietnam.

The heavy recoil of the 152mm gun is clear here as it lifts the front suspension of this Sheridan firing on Range 3 at Cu Chi on 1 February 1969. The combustible-case conventional rounds were more than adequate against any target found in Vietnam.

On 23 February 1969 troops from 1st Squadron, 11th Armored Cavalry Regiment use the M551 to probe the brush near Long Binh searching for Viet Cong. Combined arms operations such as this were a necessity in combating guerilla warfare.

"The Devil Avenges," an 11 ACR Sheridan, was photographed while operating in Vietnam in February 1969. Scarcely a month in theater and numerous changes to the vehicle have been made – including the installation of an ACAV shield on the commander's .50 caliber machine gun. (James Loop via Patton Museum)

Three days before Christmas 1969, this group of Sheridans was found at Quan Loi undergoing repair by the 185th Maintenance Battalion. In addition to the previously mentioned cooling problems, preventative maintenance of the suspension by crews was often lacking, being impaired by the extremely muddy conditions often found in Vietnam.

By the time this photo was taken, on 8 July 1969, crews had begun extensive operations with the Sheridans. This "A" Troop, 3rd Squadron, 4th Cavalry, 25th Infantry Division M551 moves across a rice paddy in search of the enemy. The improvised bustle stowage rack is overflowing with gear and ammunition boxes.

"Aretha" – sporting "Rhino Power" graffiti on the ACAV gun shield – patrols the jungle's edge. This vehicle, like many Sheridans in Vietnam, was assigned to the 11th Armored Cavalry Regiment. Crewmen often rode on the outside of the vehicles, risking small arms fire to escape the heat, and risk from land mines, that were inherent with riding inside. (Patton Museum)

Vietnam was not the only place to which the M551 was deployed in 1969. This Sheridan was photographed in early February of that year in Alaska. Assigned to "D" Company, 40th Armored Regiment, 172nd Infantry Brigade, the vehicle is taking part in Exercise "Acid Test I, Punch Card V."

As a result of various exercises in Alaska, it was determined that the Sheridan was not well-suited for operation in Arctic conditions. Here an M578 is used to recover a stalled M551 of "D" Company, 40th Armored Regiment, 172nd Infantry Brigade in February 1969.

This Sheridan served with the 2nd Platoon, C Troop, 1st Squadron, 11th Armored Cavalry Regiment operating in Vietnam in February 1969.

This Sheridan served with the 2nd Platoon, 1st Squadron, 11th Armored Cavalry Regiment. The M551 was used along the Cambodian border during 1969.

This "A" Troop, 3rd Squadron, 4th Cavalry, 25th Infantry Division, M551 sits in the mud at Landing Zone Hampton in Vietnam during a reconnaissance in force mission on 3 August 1969. The vehicle commander has lashed many M18 smoke grenades to the side of the turret for quick use. A small section of fencing has been installed on top of the surfboard, just ahead of the driver's position.

Mud, like this at Landing Zone Hampton in August 1969, did little to hamper the Sheridan's mobility directly, but it did contribute to maintenance problems. Numerous grease fittings dot the suspension components of the vehicle, but even if the crew member is willing to service them, thick mud made maintenance nearly impossible.

The day after Christmas, 1969, members of Troop "E," 2nd Squadron, 11th Cavalry, sweep the road for mines ahead of a column of M551 armored assault vehicles. Mines were a constant threat, and could wreak havoc on the aluminum-hulled Sheridans and M113 armored personnel carriers.

Faintly visible in this photo is the leading edge of the steel under belly armor that was part of the mine protective kit developed for the Sheridan. Although it negated the use of the driver's escape hatch, most crews believed this to be a worthwhile trade off for the protection the kit provided.

M551 Sheridan Add-On Armor Kit

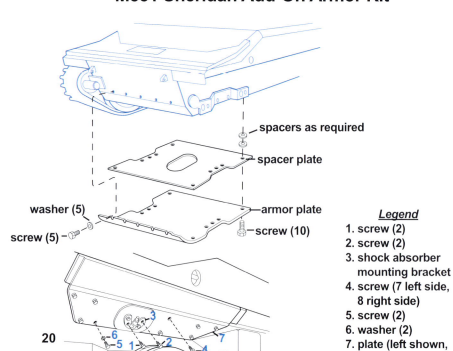

Labels: spacers as required, spacer plate, washer (5), armor plate, screw (5), screw (10)

Legend
1. screw (2)
2. screw (2)
3. shock absorber mounting bracket
4. screw (7 left side, 8 right side)
5. screw (2)
6. washer (2)
7. plate (left shown, right similar)

Members of Troop "E," 2nd Squadron, 11th Cavalry, prepare their minesweeping equipment on Christmas day 1969 beside an M551 armored assault vehicle at Fire Base "Eunice." The detector appears to be the AN/PSS-11, one of the most common such units used in Vietnam.

Many different firms produced the AN/PSS-11 mine detector. Each manufacturer assigned its own product number, including the Polan P153, P158, P190; Oregon MD-M; VP Company VP200; and Fourdee 4D5000. Notice the faded canvas cover protecting the AN/VSS-3 searchlight mounted adjacent to the Sheridan main gun.

"Hard Core 7," with "D" Troop, 3rd Squadron, 4th Cavalry, 25th Infantry Division, moves out in February 1969 on one of the first missions of the Sheridan in Vietnam. The chain link fencing mounted on the front of the vehicle was intended as a deterrent to RPGs.

"Hard Core 7" pushes its way through brush as the crew maneuvers the Sheridan into firing position in a densely wooded area near Cu Chi on 12 February 1969. The light weight of the M551, an asset when operating in mud, rendered it a much less effective "jungle buster" than the heavy M48 tanks were.

On 22 February 1969, this group of M551 Sheridans from "C" Troop, 3rd Squadron, 4th Cavalry, 25th Infantry Division were dispatched to attack suspected enemy positions only 14 kilometers from the ranges at Cu Chi where they had been training. Army strategists were eager to evaluate how the then-new Sheridan would perform in combat.

"Hard Core 7" was a Sheridan belonging to "C" Troop, 3rd Squadron, 4th Cavalry, and was assigned to the 25th Infantry Division at Tay Ninh in February 1969. Third Squadron, 4th Cavalry, along with 1st Squadron, 11th Armored Cavalry, were issued the M551s in January 1969 to replace the M48A3s with which they arrived in country.

The small size and low profile of the Sheridan meant that there was little space for stowage inside – only 29 main gun rounds were carried. The bulk of the machine gun ammunition was carried outside of the turret in standard metal ammo boxes, as on this "C" Troop, 3rd Squadron, 4th Cavalry, 25th Infantry Division vehicle.

Although the hull of the Sheridan was aluminum, the turret was steel, and accordingly, heavy. A M88 retriever is used here to pull the turret for a maintenance operation. (Rock Island Arsenal Museum)

For maintenance, the turret was placed upon a service stand, allowing easy access to all turret systems and components. (Rock Island Arsenal Museum)

In order to place the turret on the stand, maintenance personnel must first disconnect the turret from the hull. The lifting slings are attached to the designated points on the turret, and connected to the lift hoist of the M88. (Rock Island Arsenal Museum)

Once lifted clear of the turret ring, the chassis can be pulled out from under the turret, and the turret lowered to the maintenance stand. The M88 is a bit of an overkill for this job, as it is easily capable of lifting the entire Sheridan. (Rock Island Arsenal Museum)

A trio of Sheridans move out on patrol after being resupplied. The M551 mounted one of the largest caliber weapons in Vietnam, but the short barrel length meant that the rounds had a very low muzzle velocity. This made them ideal for firing on lightly protected targets, where a high velocity round, such at that fired by the Patton, could completely penetrate the target without detonating. (Rock Island Arsenal Museum)

The muzzle blast upon firing the 152mm main gun was formidable. Although originally only M409 high-explosive anti tank (HEAT) and M411-TP training rounds were developed, this was soon augmented by the M625 Canister round, which contained 10000 13 grain flechettes. The latter was widely used in Vietnam, where it could cut large swathes from both the jungle and Viet Cong infantry concentrations.

18 May 1970 found "A" Troop, 3rd Squadron, 4th Cavalry, 25th Infantry Division operating in Cambodia on search and destroy missions seeking Viet Cong supply caches. Numerous infantry personnel have hitched a ride on this Sheridan, which is already heavily festooned with sand bags, spare road wheels, crates, and other gear.

Lying across the rear hull of this 3rd Squadron, 4th Cavalry, 25th Infantry Division Sheridan is a mat or grass-weave rug used for ground cover when the crew was halted at a Night Defensive Perimeter (NDP). Atop the mat is a medium-duty vehicular towbar, used when towing a disabled vehicle. Crates, ammo boxes, and smoke grenades litter the engine deck of the vehicle as troopers ride the vehicle through the Cambodian jungle in May 1970.

These two Sheridans and M113 APCs were part of a large 11th Armored Cavalry force that pushed their way 20 miles into Cambodia to thwart the movement of men and equipment along the Ho Chi Minh Trail. This photo was taken along the road near Snoul on 4 May 1970 – the next day the Black Horse Regiment, as the 11 ACR is known, under the command of Donn A. Starry would capture and virtually obliterate Snoul.

Land mines were a constant threat. This 11ACR M551 was disabled by a land mine on Highway 7, near Snoul, Cambodia, on 8 May 1970. Moreover, when near the top speed of almost 45 MPH on the road, the M551's own heavy steel track, when thrown by an explosion, could wreak havoc on the aluminum hull components.

The same mine-disabled vehicle is seen here from in front. In the foreground is what appears to be the return roller, blown free of the vehicle by the mine blast. The mine protective kits helped protect the crews, but with the main gun rounds comprised of combustible cases, the threat of total destruction of the vehicle was high.

A Sheridan of "C" Troop, 3rd Squadron, 4th Cavalry, 11th Armored Cavalry meets a security patrol equipped with an M151 MUTT and a Dodge M37 3/4-ton cargo truck as they cross back into Vietnam from Cambodia on 27 June 1970. Typically, the M551 is heavily laden with stowage, including what appears to be five 40mm Bofors ammunition boxes. The waterproof metal boxes were no doubt obtained from one of the M42 Duster crews.

The combination of M113 ACAV and M551 provided an effective fighting team and was widely used. Both vehicles provided excellent mobility in muddy conditions, such as this road between Cambodia and Vietnam. Typically crews rode on the outside of the vehicles as here except in the most severe of conditions.

By no means were the new Sheridans shipped only to Vietnam. Large numbers also went to Europe where they faced the Soviet armor they were designed to combat. This camouflage-painted M551 from the 1st Infantry Division (Mech), passes in review at the beginning of Phase II-FTX "Certain Thrust," part of the REFORGER II (REdeployment of FORces to GERmany) exercise. REFORGER was a large-scale exercise conducted in Germany almost annually from 1969 until after the end of the Cold War.

Because of the war in Vietnam, and the lack of suitable targets for the Shillelagh missile there, not only were the missile systems removed from the initial Sheridans sent to Vietnam, others, with manufacturer's serial numbers 140-223 and 740-885, left the factory without the missile system ever having been installed. In total, over 200 Sheridans were shipped to Vietnam, including these two awaiting issue at the Class 7 area of the 625th S&S Company in June 1970.

Although the swimming ability of the M551 was seldom if ever used in Vietnam, during the REFORGER exercises it frequently came into play. Here a 1st Infantry Division Sheridan emerges from the river Main between Dippach and Rastadt in West Germany on 19 October 1970. (Patton Museum)

An M551 Armored Reconnaissance/Airborne Assault Vehicle from the 11th Armored Cavalry Regiment prepares to move out from its blockade position near Hung Loc on 23 January 1971. The loader has been equipped with a field-installed M60 machine gun, installed behind a shield from an ACAV kit. Graffiti adorns the loader's gun shield. The commander sits behind his M2 .50 caliber machine gun with shield.

Another view of the same 11ACR Sheridan – with the name "Blessed One" stenciled on the side, just to the rear of the 12F37369 registration number. The red dust of Vietnam has covered the vehicle, with heavy deposits near the seams in the flotation cover.

This Sheridan has been extensively customized. A pair of M2 Browning .50 caliber machine guns have been mounted atop the turret, and a large stowage rack has been added to the left side of the turret as well. Markings have been applied to the main gun tube, and a heavy wire tow rope is draped across the glacis. Two of the three men riding atop the turret wear the Combat Vehicle Crewmen helmet, while the third wears the standard M1 steel pot. The crew appears to have added a fifth member to the crew - the red dog riding along with them.

Sheridan G37 of Third Platoon, 11 Armored Cavalry Regiment, pulling away from the fuel and supply point in the interior of the Night Defensive Perimeter (NDP) after reprovisioning somewhere in Tan Uyen District in February, 1972. (Doug Kibbey)

With the turret of this Sheridan traversed left, the locally fabricated bustle rack installed on 2/11th M551s is exposed. Amidst the impressive array of gear that the crew has accumulated and stowed on the rear of the hull is a roll of chain link fencing, which would be erected around the vehicle at night to protect against RPGs. (Doug Kibbey)

Exhaust outlets of Sheridans in Vietnam were frequently extended with artillery powder containers, as here, to lift the fumes above the vehicle and gear; a particularly important modification when operating in tall grass or jungle. An M60 machine gun for the loader to use has been fixed on the turret. (Doug Kibbey)

This 2/11th Sheridan is being prepared to move out from an NDP. A large rubber fuel blivet has been brought in for refueling. Such collapsible rubber fuel bladders were transported by helicopter or truck, and were used to create "instant" fuel depots. Crates that held hand grenades, rations, and ammunition litter the ground. (Doug Kibbey)

G37 moves through tall grass in Military Region III (the area surrounding Saigon) in Vietnam. With the Sheridan just under 10 feet tall, grass would completely hide the vehicles in some places. (Doug Kibbey)

The crossed sabres on the side of this 11th Armored Cavalry Regiment Sheridan are symbolic of the unit's Cavalry designation. Many Sheridans and M113s of this unit operating in Vietnam carried this marking during the 1969-1970 period.

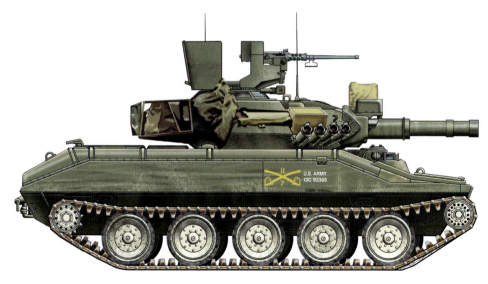

The crew of this Sheridan reprovisions their vehicle between missions. They have added a second .50 caliber machine gun, this for use by the loader, to the top of the turret, augmenting the commander's weapon. A mermite can is strapped to the back of the turret, and ammunition boxes cover the glacis. (Chris Harlow)

An M1123A1C 10-ton 6x6 tractor with M15A2 trailer transport a M551 in Vietnam. Track laying vehicles are expensive to operate on long road marches and required maintenance skyrockets. Hence, wheeled transport such as this is used to move the vehicles near the front, as well as to return worn or damaged vehicles to repair facilities. (Chris Harlow)

Shell fragments have riddled the aluminum outer flotation pod covering on this M551. The registration number identifies this Sheridan as having been built in 1970, making it one of the last of the vehicles to have been assembled. (William Powis)

This Sheridan formed part of the perimeter defense at a Fire Support Base. In such use, the canister round fired by the 152mm gun/launcher was devastatingly effective. (William Powis)

This Blackhorse M551 commander hams it up for the camera brandishing the AK-47 "souvenir" he has acquired. Brackets added to the front of the hull support the customary chain link fencing. Crates and ammo boxes cover the rear of the vehicle and turret. (Dave Orth)

G39, knocked out by a land mine, is towed back to base on its belly by a M578 recovery vehicle. The salvage crew has piled the dislodged road wheels on the hull and in the bustle basket. (Dave Orth)

The special field-produced "luggage" rack found on many 2/11th ACR Sheridans is plainly visible in this photo. Crews often carried as much extra water, oil, fuel, and ammo as they could physically place on their vehicles during operations. (William Powis)

An M88 retriever pulls into position ahead of a stowage-laden Sheridan. The smaller M578 was most often used to recover M551s, although upon occasion the massive M88 was used instead. (William Powis)

G37 is shown here after having been recovered following a mine detonation. Typically, with damage this extensive, the vehicles were DX'd ("Direct Exchange"), meaning the damaged one is turned in and a replacement/refurbished/repaired vehicle is given to the unit in exchange. The 1969-produced vehicle was repaired and returned to service, until finally being retired in 1985. (William Powis)

The bolted-on mine protective plate is visible near the bottom front of the hull. The extensive damage to the suspension is evidence of just how critically needed this additional armor was. Despite the shortcoming of thin armor, the Sheridan remained the best lightweight armored combat vehicle available, and would soldier on in further conflicts. (William Powis)

An 82nd Airborne Division M551A1 Sheridan light tank/reconnaissance vehicle is driven from Army utility landing craft 1674 (LCU 1674), upon landing at Vieques Island, Puerto Rico, during Operation OCEAN VENTURE '84. To the left is an M151 MUTT, the Army standard 1/4-ton truck of the time. The 82nd Airborne would be the last unit to use the Sheridan in a combat role. (U.S. Army)

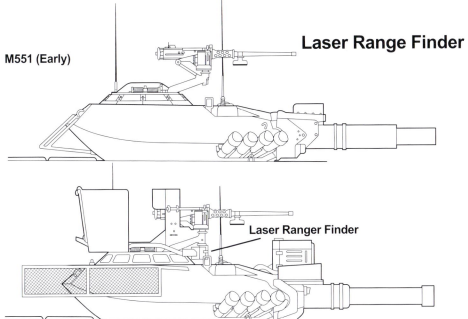

Laser Range Finder

M551 (Early)

Laser Ranger Finder

The purchase of 505 Hughes AN/VVG-1 laser range finders for installation on Sheridans was approved on 22 April 1971. Vehicles so equipped were redesignated M551A1. The laser unit beneath the machine gun mount was a key characteristic of these vehicles.

Members of the 11th Armored Cavalry deploy from an M113A1 armored personnel carrier protected by an M551A1 during an exercise near one of the many observation posts that dotted the border between East and West Germany. The camouflaged Sheridan carries black full-size markings as opposed to the small, subdued markings introduced army-wide on the later MERDC camo scheme. (U.S. Army)

The Sheridan stayed in service with the 82nd Airborne Division for a number of reasons – this is one of them. The vehicle could be transported via C-130 Hercules aircraft to primitive airfields as seen here during Exercise OCEAN VENTURE '84. It could even be airdropped. (U.S. Army)

Members of the 11th Armored Cavalry deploy around an M551A1 Sheridan Armored Reconnaissance/Airborne Assault Vehicle while guarding the border between East and West Germany. The Sheridan was developed to counter the massive buildup of Soviet armor during the Cold War. (U.S. Army)

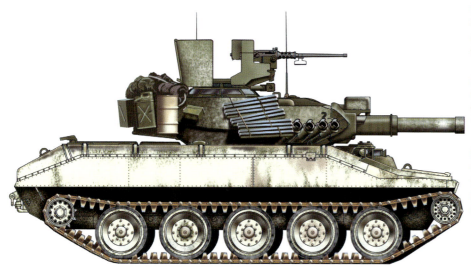

(Top) When the 3/73rd armor deployed to Saudi Arabia in 1990 for Desert Shield, they brought with them their Sheridans wearing three-color NATO camouflage. As a field expedient the vehicles were smeared with mud to better blend them into the desert terrain.

(Middle) The only combat air drop of the Sheridan occurred during Operation Just Cause – when eight vehicles were successfully air dropped into Panama, to augment four covertly airlifted into the country. This vehicle carries the markings of one of the Third Battalion, "C" Company 3/73rd Sheridans involved in this operation.

(Bottom) The M551A1(TTS) vehicles that the 3/73 rode into combat with during Operation Desert Storm had been freshly reconditioned at Anniston Army Depot. During the depot service they were painted with CARC Desert Tan FS595B 33446, also known as Tan 686 or Tan 686A. The chevron markings on the side of this Sheridan indicate it is B Company, 3rd Platoon vehicle.

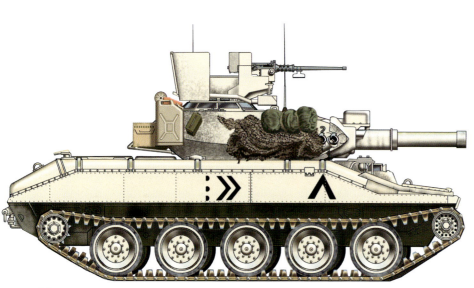

In March of 1988 President Ronald Reagan mobilized U.S. Task Force Dragon/Golden Pheasant, consisting of the 7th Light Infantry Division and elements of the 82nd Airborne Division that landed at Palmerola Air Base, Honduras. The no-notice live-fire training exercise successfully discouraged Nicaraguan forces from entering Honduras. This M551A1 Sheridan from the 3rd Battalion, 73rd Armor, 82nd Airborne Division was among those deployed, and displays the new smoke discharger configuration. (U.S. Army)

Post-Vietnam

The Sheridan was designed for a crew of four: a driver, who was seated in the front center of the hull, and a three-man turret crew consisting of the commander, gunner, and loader. As originally delivered, the gunner was at a decided disadvantage as the original sighting system left much to be desired.

In an effort to remedy this problem, in 1971 Hughes Aircraft was contracted to supply the AN/VVG1 laser rangefinder for use on the Sheridan. Vehicles with this system installed were reclassified as M551A1. They could be visually distinguished from the earlier models by the laser installed beneath the commander's machine gun mount. Internally, an M127A1 telescope replaced the M127 telescope previously mounted at the gunner's position.

In 1977 a Product Improvement Program (PIP) was launched to update the Sheridan and address certain deficiencies found in combat. The original tow lugs, made of aluminum and welded to the hull, were prone to being torn off in operation. The PIP package included steel tow lugs, which penetrated the hull and were bolted to steel backing plates. A more robust drive sprocket was also installed, and the slave starting receptacle was relocated from inside the vehicle to a position on the outside of the hull front.

Internally, the tired aluminum-blocked 6V53T Detroit Diesel engines were replaced with newer versions with cast iron blocks, improved turbosuperchargers, and an improved throttle control. The result was an unfortunate increase in weight, but a gain in improved reliability, increased performance, and a markedly less noticeable exhaust plume. Still later, newer-style cluster smoke grenade launchers replaced the original groups, and the M240 7.62mm coaxial machine gun replaced the original-type M219 machine gun.

Operation Just Cause, the US overthrow of Panamanian dictator Manuel Noriega in December 1989, was the first combat use of the Sheridan since America's withdrawal from Vietnam. The Sheridans provided the needed punch to blast through the best Panamanian defenses. (U.S. Army via Michael Green)

Two members of the 82nd Airborne Division repair the left drive sprocket on an M551 Sheridan light tank parked at the international airport following Operation Just Cause, the U.S. invasion of Panama. Fourteen Sheridans were deployed – four landed by C-5 and ten air dropped, although two of the ten did not survive the landing. (U.S. Army)

M551 Sheridans were among the first U.S. armored vehicles to arrive in Saudi Arabia in support of Operation Desert Shield in 1990. C-5 Galaxies flew them into theater still wearing their European camouflage. Designed to be carried by the C-130 and other smaller aircraft, the M551 was no challenge for the mammoth Galaxy. (Department of Defense)

The 56 M551A1 Sheridans operated by the 3rd Battalion, 73rd Airborne Armor Regiment, 82nd Airborne Division in Operation Desert Storm were specially modified with the installation of the Tank Thermal Sight (TTS) from the M60A3 at Anniston Army Depot, which concurrently overhauled and painted the vehicles. The modified vehicles replaced those already in theater during November and December 1990. As the air war began, they were repositioned in theater via C-130H Hercules, seen being loaded here. (Department of Defense)

The Basic Issue Items (BII) of an M551A1(TTS) during operation Desert Storm included both conventional munitions (foreground) and the Shillelagh missile. The protective covers for the combustible cartridge cases were to be removed just before loading the rounds. This Sheridan and its crew were attached to Company A, 3rd Battalion, 73rd Airborne Armor Regiment, 82nd Airborne Division. This was the only unit still operating the Sheridan by the time of the Gulf War. (Department of Defense)

This crew of an M551A1(TTS) Sheridan fresh from overhaul and modification takes their new mount to the firing range during Operation Desert Shield. Live-fire drills such as this honed the skills of the men, and made them familiar with their vehicle and surroundings. Thus when Desert Shield evolved into Desert Storm the Sheridans were notably effective, despite the newest of the vehicles being 22 years old. (Department of Defense)

A soldier mans an M-224 60mm mortar as an M551A1 Sheridan patrols a section of desert during an exercise, part of Operation Desert Shield. Judging from the paint scheme, this is likely one of the first such vehicles to arrive in theater, redeployed from Europe and hastily smeared with mud in order to blend into the desert. (Department of Defense)

An M55A1 crew from the 82nd Airborne Division takes time out on a trail during their rotation at the Joint Readiness Training Center in 1996. This was the next to last year that the 82nd would field the Sheridan, despite no suitable replacement having been found. (Department of Defense)

An M55A1 on patrol in support of the 82nd Airborne at the Joint Readiness Training Center. The blank firing adapter on the commander's M2 Heavy Barrel (HB) machine gun is evident, as is the amber strobe light that flashes several times, indicating a simulated near miss on the vehicle, or continuously for a faux "kill." (Department of Defense)

The last bastion for the Sheridan was at the National Training Center. Among the uses found for the vehicles there was as transport for referee and control personnel. Vehicles put to this use, such as this one, had their gun-launcher removed and additional electronics equipment installed. (Department of Defense).

Other Sheridans were visually modified (VisMod) with special kits to resemble Warsaw Pact-type vehicles and served as the opposing force. Ironically, the opposing force crewing such vehicles today – like this BMP look-alike – is the 11 Armored Cavalry Regiment – the same unit that employed the Sheridan so effectively in Vietnam. (Department of Defense)

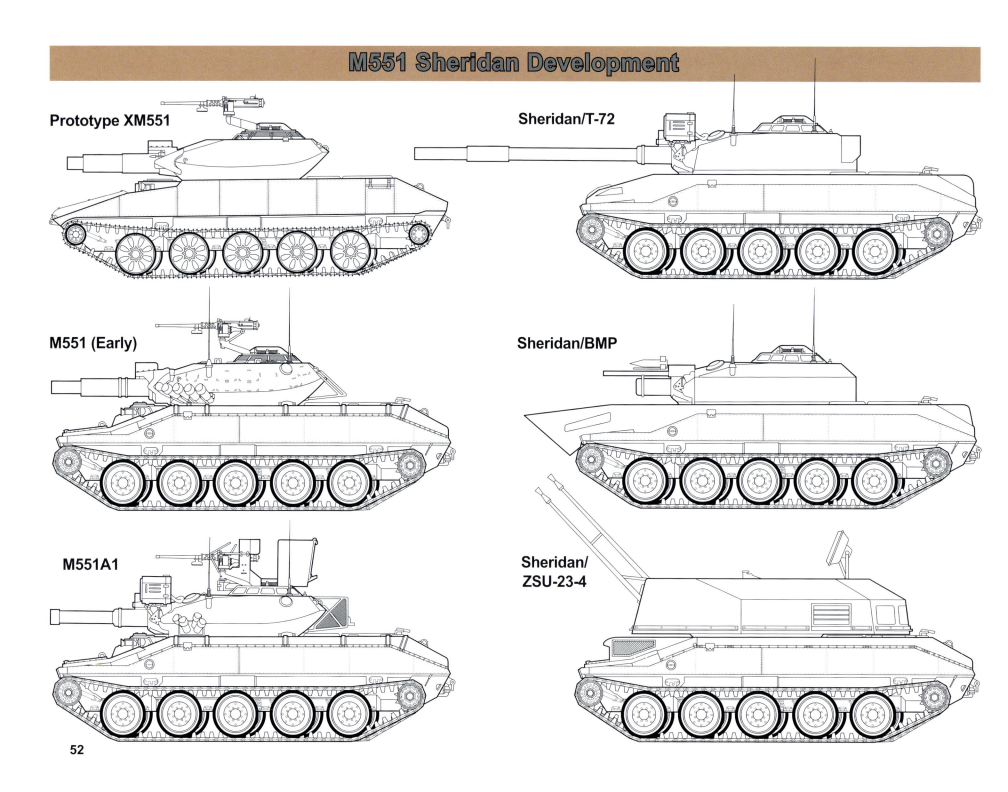

A right front view of M551A1 Sheridan modified to look like a T-72 Soviet tank. The cutouts in the front fenders provide visibility to the driver. The tank is used by the 177th Armored Brigade, which until the 11 ACR assumed their role as an opposing force in October 1994, provided such personnel during exercises at the National Training Center. (Department of Defense)

This faux Soviet BMP-1 is actually a visually modified M551A1 Sheridan. Sheetmetal, plywood and fiberglass are primary components of the kits used to create these training vehicles, which are redesignated M551NTC. These vehicles are fitted with sensors that detect "hits" by opposing forces, and fire "guns" against them. (Department of Defense)

Panama and Desert Storm

During 1978, the Sheridan was withdrawn for use except for those assigned to 3rd Battalion (Airborne), 73rd Armor, 82nd Airborne Division. Equipped with the Sheridan in 1969, this unit had at that time been known as the 4th Battalion (Airborne), 68th Armor. The bulk of the remainder of the vehicles were initially placed in long-term storage. Three hundred Sheridans were dispatched to the National Training Center at Fort Irwin, California, however. There they were equipped with visual modification (VISMOD) kits so that they would resemble a variety of Soviet-bloc vehicles. Such modified vehicles were designated the M551NTC and used in training.

In December 1989 the Sheridan once again answered the call to arms as the U.S. embarked upon Operation Just Cause. Just Cause was the name of the swift operation used to depose Panamanian dictator Manuel Noriega.

Prior to the operation, four Sheridans were secretly flown into Panama, their bumper codes being changed to indicate assignment to 5th Infantry Division (and their crews wearing like insignia), a unit that routinely rotated through the Canal Zone for training. Once the operation began, additional Sheridans were airdropped into Panama. The importance of the Sheridan to the success of this operation is evidenced by the frequent reference to the vehicles in operational reports.

Just prior to Desert Storm some of these vehicles were equipped with the Tank Thermal Sight as used in the M60A3. Sheridans so equipped were designated M551A1(TTS) – and were the most accurate versions of the vehicle fielded. This modification was carried out at the Anniston Army Depot, which at the same time adapted the driver's night viewing system from the Bradley fighting vehicle for use on the Sheridan. So equipped, the Sheridan once again proved its worth on the battlefield. This would, however, be the final combat deployment of the now three-decades-old vehicle, and even the M551NTC variants were soon retired.

Other M551NTC Sheridans were modified to resemble a Soviet ZSU-23-4 self-propelled anti-aircraft gun system. The visual modifications were very effective, especially in low-light situations such as this. (Department of Defense)

By 2003 the Sheridan was phased out of use even for training purposes. Some vehicles were preserved in combat configuration, others scrapped or dumped at sea. A handful, such as this M551NTC resembling a Soviet T-72 main battle tank, are preserved in VisMod configuration. (Department of Defense)

After the fall of Iron Curtain, actual Eastern Bloc vehicles became available for use at the NTC, further numbering the Sheridan's days. Here, two variant M551NTC Sheridan light armored tanks from the 11th Armored Cavalry Regiment roll by Colonel John Rosenberger, left, on an M551 Sheridan and Lieutenant Colonel Michael Chambers on a Russian BMP-1 armored personnel vehicle. (Department of Defense)

M551 Sheridan MERDC Camouflage

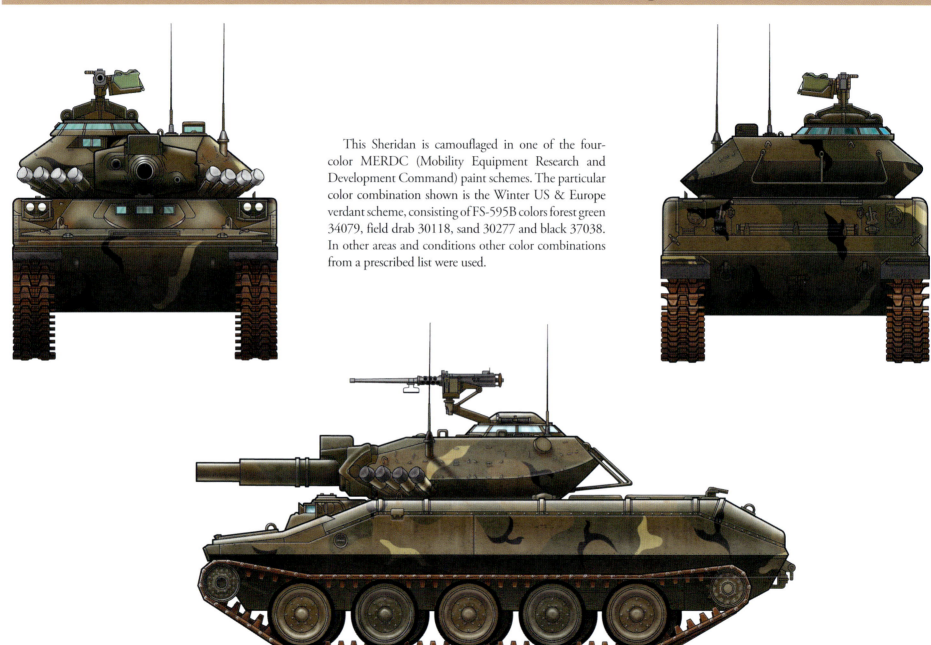

This Sheridan is camouflaged in one of the four-color MERDC (Mobility Equipment Research and Development Command) paint schemes. The particular color combination shown is the Winter US & Europe verdant scheme, consisting of FS-595B colors forest green 34079, field drab 30118, sand 30277 and black 37038. In other areas and conditions other color combinations from a prescribed list were used.

M551 Sheridan MERDC Camouflage

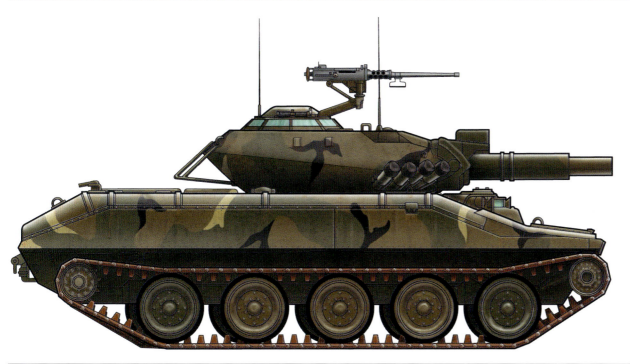
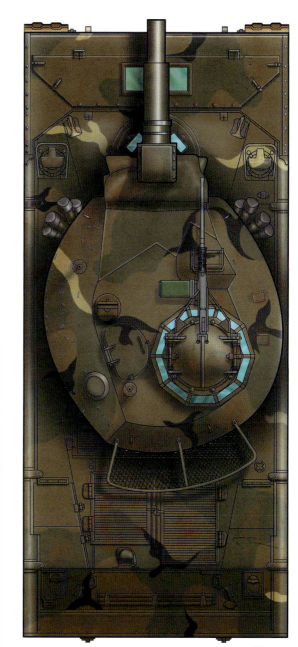

Condition	Color Distribution FS595A			
	45%	45%	5%	5%
Color number	1	3	3	
Winter U.S. & Europe—verdant	Forest Green 34079	Field Drab 30118	Sand 30277	Black 37038
Snow-temperature w/trees & shrubs	Forest Green 34079	White 37875	Sand 30277	Black 37038
Snow-temperature w/open terrain	White 37875	Field Drab 30118	Sand 30277	Black 37038
Summer U.S. & Europe—verdant	Forest Green 34079	Light Green 34151	Sand 30277	Black 37038
Tropics—verdant	Forest Green 34079	Dark Green 34102	Light Green 34151	Black 37038
Gray desert	Sand 30277	Field Drab 30118	Earth Yellow 30257	Black 37038
Red desert	Earth Red 30117	Earth Yellow 30257	Sand 30277	Black 37038
Winter Arctic	White 37875	White 37875	White 37875	White 37875

M551A1 Sheridan NATO Camouflage

The standard NATO three-color camouflage pattern is shown here. The position of each of the colors is specific, there is no random placement. The colors used in this pattern are 383 green FS-595B 34094, 383 brown FS-595B 30051 and black, FS-595B 37030.

M551A1 Sheridan NATO Camouflage

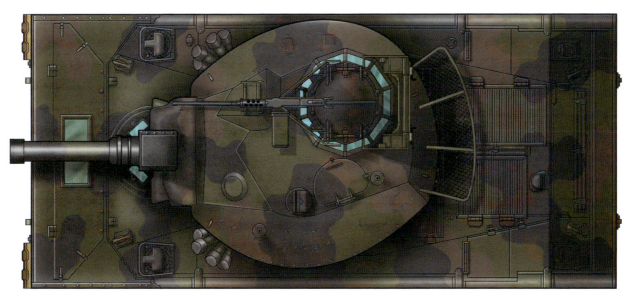

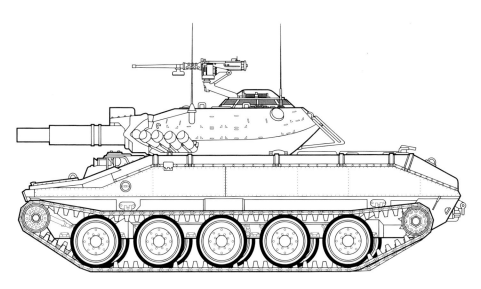
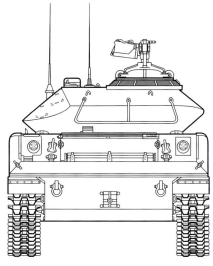

Specifications
M551 Sheridan

Crew........................Four
Length....................20.43 Feet
Width......................9.25 Feet
Height.....................9.66 Feet
Weight...................34,899 Pounds

Armament
Main........................152 mm gun/missile launcher
Secondary...............One 7.62 mm coaxial machine gun, One .50 caliber M2 Browning on commander's cupola
Engine.....................Detroit-Diesel 6V-53T 300 hp turbocharged diesel engine
Speed......................43.5 mph
Range......................373 miles

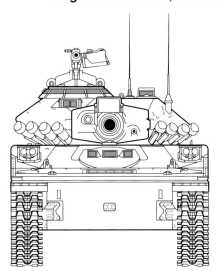
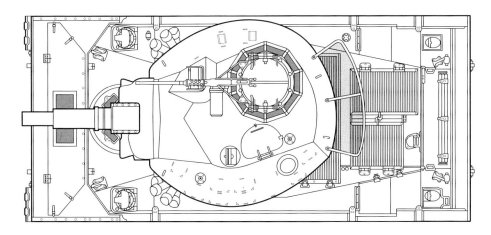